Earth-Friendly Food

Gillian Gosman

PowerKiDS press.

New York

Published in 2011 by The Rosen Publishing Group, Inc.
29 East 21st Street, New York, NY 10010

First Edition

Editor: Joanne Randolph
Book Design: Kate Laczynski

Photo Credits: Cover Jupiterimages/BananaStock/Thinkstock; p. 4 (top) © www.iStockphoto.com/Dan Moore; pp. 4 (bottom), 20 (top) Ben Bloom/Getty Images; p. 5 © www.iStockphoto.com/Silvia Jansen; p. 6 BananaStock/Thinkstock; p. 7 Stockbyte/Thinkstock; p. 8 © www.iStockphoto.com/Dave Hughes; p. 9 © www.iStockphoto.com/Scott David Patterson; pp. 10, 15, 25 Shutterstock.com; p. 11 © http://en.wikipedia.org/wiki/File:USDA_organic_seal.svg; pp. 12–13 Tim Graham/Getty Images; p. 14 Cavan Images/Getty Images; p. 16 © www.iStockphoto.com/Fertnig; p. 17 Hemera/Thinkstock; pp. 18–19 Jochen Sand/Digital Vision/Thinkstock; p. 20 (bottom) © www.iStockphoto.com/Chris Price; p. 21 John Howard/Getty Images; p. 22 © www.iStockphoto.com/Amy Riley; p. 23 Dag Sundberg/Getty Images; p. 24 © www.iStockphoto.com/Joerg Reimann; pp. 26–27 © www.iStockphoto.com/seraficus; p. 28 Jupiterimages/Creatas/Thinkstock; p. 29 Jupiterimages/Getty Images; p. 30 Tim Sloan/AFP/Getty Images.

Library of Congress Cataloging-in-Publication Data

Gosman, Gillian.
 Earth-friendly food / by Gillian Gosman. — 1st ed.
   p. cm. — (How to be earth friendly)
 Includes index.
 ISBN 978-1-4488-2589-9 (library binding) — ISBN 978-1-4488-2767-1 (pbk.) — ISBN 978-1-4488-2768-8 (6-pack)
 1. Natural foods. 2. Sustainable living. 3. Environmental responsibility. I. Title.
 GE195.G674 2011
 641.3'02—dc22
                          2010034685

Manufactured in the United States of America

CPSIA Compliance Information: Batch #WW11PK: For Further Information contact Rosen Publishing, New York, New York at 1-800-237-9932

CONTENTS

What Is Earth-Friendly Food?

Organic produce, such as these vegetables, is produce that is grown without harmful pesticides. It is also harvested and brought to stores in ways that will not hurt Earth.

The terms Earth-friendly or green food can mean different things to different people. For some, it describes food that is grown or raised through **sustainable** farming. Sustainable farmers work to keep the soil naturally rich and strong. They also try to keep nearby waterways free from

Some people think food grown locally is the friendliest to Earth. Local food does not need to travel far, so trucks that carry it use less gas and less pollution gets into the air.

pesticides. For them, Earth-friendly food is food grown or raised without **chemicals** and without animal cages.

Some people are interested in how their food gets from the farm to their table. For them, green food might be food that is made near where they live. This lessens fuel use and air pollution from the trucks that carry the food to the store. Everyone interested in green food is also interested in keeping the natural world safe.

This lettuce is being grown on an organic farm. Many people believe that food that has been treated with fewer chemicals is better for our bodies.

Science has done great things for food. We can make more food than ever before and ship it around the world. The science of food is not all good, though. The technology used to make food

Many of the foods on grocery store shelves are processed foods. These foods last a long time. The chemicals that let them do that are not always healthy to eat, though.

bigger, brighter, and cheaper can hurt our health and Earth. Many people in the Earth-friendly food movement are worried about what goes into food. They do not think **additives**, **synthetic** sweeteners, and overly **refined** grains and oils are good for us. Other people worry about how farmers work the land, factories package the food, and planes and trucks carry the food around the world.

People in the green food movement are also concerned about bovine growth **hormone**, or BGH. BGH is a chemical that cattle make naturally. Scientists figured out how to make it, too.

Here a worker sprays pesticides on crops. The worker is wearing special clothes and a mask. This is because these chemicals are not good for people!

The name "rBGH" stands for "recombinant bovine growth hormone." "Recombinant" means it is living material created artificially, or not by nature.

Many people believe that rBGH causes cancer or other health problems in people who drink milk from the cows that have been treated with this hormone.

Now dairy farmers give this synthetic hormone, called rBGH, to their cattle to make them grow larger and produce more milk. Cattle given rBGH are more likely to get sick, though. Some people are worried that the hormone might harm the people who drink the milk, too.

Organic farmers do not use chemicals that hurt the environment. They use natural fertilizers and pesticides instead.

Another hot topic is synthetic pesticides and **fertilizers**. These chemicals are used to kill pests and make the soil more productive. In the long run, though, these chemicals actually destroy nutrients and weaken the soil. Rain also washes these chemicals under ground and into rivers, lakes, and oceans. There they kill plant and animal life.

9

Go Organic!

There are more organic products on grocery store shelves than ever before. When you choose organic products, you are choosing to help Earth!

Many people believe that **organic** food looks, tastes, and serves your body better. They also believe organic farming practices do less harm to the environment. These people buy organic products instead of those made using more harmful practices. Organic products include food, cleaning supplies, clothes, toys, and so much more.

To keep the American shopper safe, the U.S. Department of Agriculture (USDA) is in charge of regulating, or watching over, the organic food industry. Farmers who want to sell their goods with the "organic" label must be accredited, or recognized, as organic by the USDA.

The USDA looks for three things on farms that want to be accredited as organic. First, it checks how the food was produced. Were any synthetic pesticides or fertilizers used

Look for this seal on the foods you buy. This label lets you know for sure that a food is organic.

during growing? How were the crops harvested? How was **livestock** treated? Were animals given organic food and allowed to go outside? Were the animals given **antibiotics** or growth hormones? Next, the USDA checks how the food was processed

Earth-friendly farmers of livestock let their cattle move more freely. Compare these cows on an organic farm to those seen on page 8.

and handled between the time it was harvested and when it appeared in your grocery store. For each step of production, the USDA has decided what is considered organic practice. There are rules about what can be said on a food label. The USDA decides which foods can be labeled

"100 percent organic" and which cannot. There are fines for companies that label their products incorrectly or dishonestly.

Small, organic farms do not need a lot of land to be cleared.

In the Earth-friendly food movement, "sustainable" describes food that is produced without using up natural resources or polluting the soil, air, and water with human-made waste. Most of the food in the United States is grown or raised on large factory farms. These farms use up resources and pollute our natural environment.

Some organic farmers raise animals other than cattle, chickens, and pigs. Llamas, such as these, have soft coats that can be shaved and used to make fine yarn.

Sustainable farms are usually small and family owned. Many sustainable farms grow a mix of crops and raise small groups of more than one kind of animal. They may also use their crops to make other goods, such as jam, bread, and dried fruit, to sell at markets and restaurants.

Sustainable farmers can work to keep the environment safe in several ways. They can guard the health of the soil by planting no-till crops. When the ground is tilled, or dug

Factory farms produce so much waste! Fertilizers break down, letting a dangerous gas called ammonia into the air. Animals produce waste that is held in huge open-air lagoons.

up, for planting, it dries out and erodes. No-till crops are grown from seeds that do not need to be buried under the soil.

Sustainable farmers can keep waterways on and near their farms safe, too. They can do this by using as few synthetic pesticides and fertilizers as

This is an animal-waste lagoon. Some people worry that leaks from these lagoons can get into the water supply. The gases from the lagoons can hurt Earth, too.

possible and by planting trees and bushes that catch and hold water in the soil.

Lastly, sustainable farmers can work toward **biodiversity**, or a mix of plants and animals, on their farms. This way different nutrients are being taken out of and put back into the soil. They can plant trees and bushes that draw useful bugs, birds, and bats to them, too.

Sustainable farmers often decide to grow plants that are native to their area. These kinds of plants do not need a lot of extra water or chemicals to grow well.

Love the Local Stuff

A "locavore" is a person who eats goods grown or raised close to home. This new word was created by the localism movement, which is another Earth-friendly food trend. Locavores are worried about the **carbon footprint** made by the refrigerated trucks and planes used to carry food to the grocery store. They are also concerned with the additives used to keep food fresh for those long rides.

Some locavores choose to eat only foods that are made within 50 to 100 miles (80–160 km) from their homes. Doing this means the selection of foods available is limited.

Think of how many plastic and paper bags your family has thrown away after your trips to the grocery store. Reusable shopping bags cut down on waste.

These locavores will buy only fruits and vegetables that are in season, or being harvested by farmers at the moment. That said, the fruits and vegetables locavores buy are fresher and tastier than almost anything they can buy from far away.

If you take local to the next level, you need only step outside your door. You can plant a great vegetable and herb garden even in the smallest of spaces.

Planting a garden in your backyard is fun and rewarding. Your family will also enjoy eating all the fresh fruits and vegetables you grow!

Cooperate!

A cooperative is any group that comes together to do more than it could alone. There are housing cooperatives, health-care cooperatives, and credit cooperatives for your banking needs. A food cooperative, also called a food co-op, is a business created by workers or customers to sell natural, organic, or locally grown foods. There are more

Some food cooperatives get produce from a community garden. In a community garden, neighbors work together to grow produce that everyone shares.

than 350 food co-ops in North America.

Most food co-ops are retail stores, or businesses where the public can go to buy their groceries. However, to shop there, you may have to be a member. This

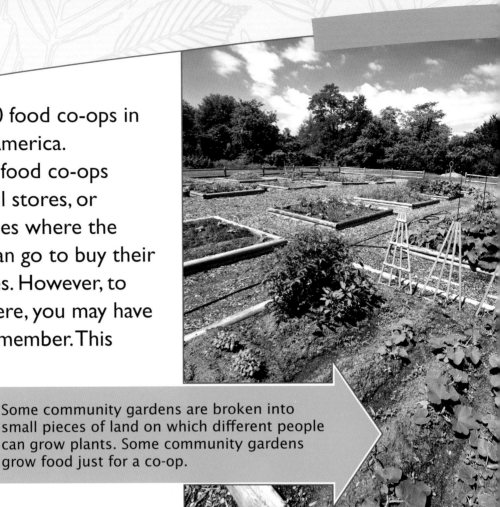

Some community gardens are broken into small pieces of land on which different people can grow plants. Some community gardens grow food just for a co-op.

sometimes means you have to pay a fee to join or work a certain number of hours in the store. Food co-ops often offer classes, information about food production and preparation, and other resources for the community.

The members of a food co-op cooperate, or work together, to run the store because they believe in the food sold there. The members govern, or make the rules for, the co-op and often use the strength of their numbers to make changes in their communities.

This man works at his local food co-op. Is there a food co-op near you?

Not Just Veggies

Many people think free-range chickens are healthier. However, not all free-range animals live in good conditions.

Livestock is an important part of a sustainable farm. On most sustainable farms, fields are allowed to lie fallow, or unplanted, every once in a while. This allows the soil to grow rich with nutrients. Livestock, such as cattle and sheep, can graze on, or eat, the grasses on these fields. This way the land is still being used for food production. Grass-fed livestock that is allowed to move freely outdoors is healthier than livestock kept in crowded barns and fed processed grains. The same is true for poultry, or chickens, turkeys, ducks, and geese. These birds are raised for their eggs and meat. Poultry that is allowed to move freely in a field is called free range. The eggs and meat that come from them are labeled "free range," too.

Pigs that are kept in pens do not exercise their muscles as much as they should. This can make them unhealthy.

Many waterways have been overfished, meaning the population of one or more kinds of fish has been almost destroyed by human fishing. For this reason, many kinds of fish are now grown on farms. Sometimes these fish are raised in nets on the open sea. Other times they are in large, crowded, indoor tanks.

Fish farms were started because demand for fish in the wild led to overfishing. However, fish raised in farms are crowded and can become sick.

The Earth-friendly food movement has **criticized** fish farming. Fish farms produce a lot of waste. They also allow for the spread of diseases among the fish, which must then be treated with antibiotics. Many people in the green food movement buy only fish caught in the wild.

If the Earth-friendly food movement matters to you, you will need to become a smart shopper. You will want to learn the USDA's label language so you understand what you are buying.

Only goods labeled "100 percent organic" with the USDA seal are made of only organic ingredients. The label "organic" means that the USDA has established

Since organic foods are popular, many companies say they are organic when they are not. You need to read labels carefully and look for the USDA seal.

that at least **95 percent** of the ingredients in a product are organic. A product with at least **70 percent** organic ingredients can include the words "made with organic ingredients" on its label. If less than 70 percent of the ingredients are organic, the food maker cannot say the product is organic.

Organically Grown

MARKET

AND PROCESSED IN ACCORDANCE WITH THE CALIFORNIA ORGANIC FOODS ACT OF 1990

These apples were organically grown to meet California's standards for organic foods. The USDA has accredited some state agencies to certify foods as organic.

When First Lady Michelle Obama decided to plant an herb and vegetable garden on the lawn of the White House, she asked a group of local fifth graders to help her do it.

The Earth-friendly food movement is gaining ground. Young people are playing an important part in it. You can do your share by planting a garden of your own, visiting a farmer's market, and buying goods from organic, sustainable farms.

GLOSSARY

additives (A-duh-tivz) Things that are added to products to make them last longer or look or taste better.

antibiotics (an-tee-by-AH-tiks) Things that kill bacteria.

biodiversity (by-oh-dih-VER-sih-tee) The number of different types of living things that are found in a certain place on Earth.

carbon footprint (KAR-bun FUHT-print) The amount of carbon dioxide a person or community creates from the actions they take and the products they use.

chemicals (KEH-mih-kulz) Materials that can be mixed with other matter to cause changes.

criticized (KRIH-tuh-syzd) Found fault with.

fertilizers (FUR-tuh-ly-zerz) Chemicals or matter put in soil to help crops grow.

hormone (HOR-mohn) A chemical in a body that controls the activities of certain parts of the body.

livestock (LYV-stok) Animals, most often cows, raised on a farm for food.

organic (or-GA-nik) Made without human-made chemicals, pesticides, or medicines.

pesticides (PES-tuh-sydz) Poisons used to kill pests.

refined (rih-FYND) Purified through mechanical or chemical processes.

sustainable (suh-STAYN-uh-bel) Able to be kept going, using a resource that can be renewed.

synthetic (sin-THEH-tik) Something that is not made in nature, human-made.

INDEX

WEB SITES

Due to the changing nature of Internet links, PowerKids
Press has developed an online list of Web sites related
to the subject of this book. This site is updated regularly.
Please use this link to access the list:
www.powerkidslinks.com/hbef/food/